# ZLATAN IBRAHIMOVIĆ

# THE ULTIMATE FAN BOOK

### SECOND EDITION

Adrian Besley

CARLTON
BOOKS

# CONTENTS

| | |
|---|---|
| INTRODUCTION | 6 |
| THE EARLY YEARS | 8 |
| HIS FIRST CLUBS | 10 |
| GOING PROFESSIONAL | 12 |
| AJAX ACE | 14 |
| SWEDISH SHINING STAR | 18 |
| JUVE MARKSMAN | 20 |
| ZLATAN'S GREAT GOALS – PART ONE | 24 |
| WORLD CUP ADVENTURE | 26 |
| ZLATAN'S SUPER SKILLS | 28 |
| IN RONALDO'S FOOTSTEPS | 30 |
| ZLATAN'S LIFE OUTSIDE FOOTBALL | 34 |
| WORLD CLASS | 36 |
| BARÇA BOUND | 38 |
| THE RETURN TO ITALY | 40 |
| ZLATAN'S GREAT GOALS – PART TWO | 44 |
| ZLATAN'S TEAMMATES | 46 |
| THE PRIDE OF PARIS | 48 |
| ZLATAN'S GREAT GOALS – PART THREE | 50 |
| THE GOAL OF THE CENTURY | 52 |
| CAPTAIN ZLATAN | 54 |
| ZLATAN SAYS... | 56 |
| ZLATAN – THE COACHES' VIEW | 58 |
| AMAZING ZLATAN | 60 |
| CREDITS | 62 |

# INTRODUCTION

Zlatan. Everyone knows him by his first name. It's a name that conjures up a host of images. Sequences of dribbles, flicks, volleys, stepovers and fierce shots. Snippets of outrageous skill and jaw-dropping agility. Remember the incredible scorpion kick that stunned Italy in Euro 2004? The left-footed volley that won the *Scudetto* for Inter Milan? Or the bicycle-kick goal against England that was acclaimed as the "greatest goal ever scored"?

Zlatan's is a classic tale of rags to riches. A story of how the immigrant's son from the ghetto rose to enjoy the millionaire superstar lifestyle. Zlatan Ibrahimović's journey has taken him from Malmö in Sweden to some of the greatest clubs in Europe. He finished top of every domestic league he played in between 2003 and 2011. He has won titles with five different sides in four countries.

Through a combination of natural talent, hours of practice and learning from the best coaches in the world, Zlatan took his place among the elite footballers on the planet. For over 10 years he has been in high demand – more money has been spent on his transfer fees (around €180 million) than any other player – with both established and aspiring clubs. There are no short cuts to building a successful side, but signing Zlatan definitely increases your chances. Ajax, Juventus, Inter, AC Milan and Paris Saint-Germain all had lean times before the Swede was added to their squad. With him in their team, they went on to become champions

In 2013, in Sweden, a new verb was added to the dictionary – "to Zlatan". It means "to dominate". Similarly, the French have adopted the word "to Zlatan" as slang for "achieving something easily". Different meanings, but the same idea – this is a man who leaves a unique impression on a football match, a man who puts the beauty into the beautiful game.

Another goal! Zlatan is Sweden's all-time leading goalscorer with 56 goals.

On his way to a second consecutive league championship with French club Paris Saint-Germain in 2014-15.

# THE EARLY YEARS

**The district of Rosengård in Malmö, Sweden, lies deep in the heart of Zlatan Ibrahimović. This is where the young Zlatan first displayed the skills that would one day astonish the world...**

On the patch of ground where Zlatan Ibrahimović began his incredible footballing journey there is now a modern, floodlit, five-a-side pitch. From a very early age, Zlatan could be found kicking his ball around the gravel courtyard between the housing blocks, hoping to be allowed to play with the older boys. Twenty years later, he helped pay for a new pitch to be built – and in honour of the neighbourhood's local hero it was named Zlatan Court.

Zlatan Ibrahimović was born on October 3, 1981 in Rosengård, a district of Malmö, the third largest city in Sweden. Rosengård is a poor area where immigrants from many parts of the globe have settled and started a new life. Zlatan's parents left the former Yugoslavia for Sweden in the late 1970s, but a few years later, when he was only two years old, they divorced.

Zlatan lived with his mother, his sister, two half-sisters and a half-brother in a small fourth-floor flat. When he wasn't at school, he kept out of the way, spending hours kicking a ball around the courtyard. When he was five he got his first football boots. They were the cheapest pair in the bargain bin at a Malmö supermarket, but it didn't matter: Zlatan was on his way.

At the age of 10, Zlatan moved in with his father and began to share his dad's interest in boxing, and Muhammad Ali in particular. Zlatan loved the great boxer's upbeat, positive attitude, but realized that boasting "I'm the greatest" was nothing if you didn't have the talent to back it up. So Zlatan worked on his football skills, playing for hours and hours after school, even when it was really too dark to carry on.

Like all his friends, Zlatan loved to learn the tricks, feints and skills of street football. He'd work on his ball control and new ways of slipping past defenders until he could try them out for real in the courtyard matches. He was still pretty small for his age in those early years, but often he still managed to bamboozle older and bigger players. Now the local youth teams were beginning to notice the little lad with the flicks and tricks.

Before long, Zlatan's amazing journey would begin, but he always remembers how these courtyard games set him on his way.

**Zlatan never gave up on his dream of becoming a professional footballer.**

## ZLATAN FACT:

As a young boy, Zlatan struggled with a strong lisp. His school sent him to a speech therapist to help lose it.

The Rosengård estate in Malmö, Sweden, where Zlatan spent his early life. He got his first football boots when he was five.

The football pitches where Zlatan tirelessly practised were renamed "Zlatan Court" in his honour. He returned to the area in 2007 to help coach budding footballers.

NNS MITT HJÄRTA.
NNS MIN HISTORIA.
INNS MITT SPEL.

DET VIDARE.

# HIS FIRST CLUBS

**There were plenty of local teams chasing the fiery young lad with a bagful of flicks and tricks, but could he transfer his skills from the courtyard matches to the grass pitches and make it as a professional?**

When he was seven, Zlatan started to play for neighbourhood clubs. The boys he played with were often two or more years older than him. He sometimes turned out for the Rosengård youth team, Malmö Anadolu BI (MABI), but within a couple of years he moved to FBK Balkan. This local team had been formed by Yugoslavian immigrants and the coach, Ivica Kurtovic, was a Bosnian like Zlatan's father.

In an interview in Sweden's *Offside* magazine, Kurtovic remembered the still-small boy. "Many of the boys could have been as good as Zlatan. What tipped the scale in his favour was his attitude to the game. A few of them missed training, but Zlatan wanted more. I often saw him in his garden playing football on his own."

But the young Zlatan had a fiery temper. He argued with the opposition, referees, his teammates and even his coaches. Once he decided he could do a better job than the goalie and went in goal. On other occasions he would storm off and play for MABI or BK Flagg, another local team.

FBK, however, appreciated the strong-willed lad's skills and always welcomed him back. Kurtovic tells the story of an under-12s match. Zlatan had been made a substitute as a punishment, but with FBK trailing 4–0 at half-time they sent him on. He scored eight and they went on to win 8–5!

In 1994, when he was 13, Zlatan joined Malmö FF's youth team. Malmö already had an excellent team and they weren't as tolerant of Zlatan's dribbling and tricks as FBK had been. Zlatan often found himself sitting on the subs' bench. The next season Malmö won the junior league. As a sub, Zlatan contributed some important goals and assists, but he didn't feel he was an important part of the team.

Would Zlatan make it as a professional? It was make or break time. He gave up school and dedicated himself to a football career. At home, he was determined to master the step-overs and shots of his hero, the Brazilian Ronaldo. And, on the training field, he applied himself as never before.

Having now grown several inches, Zlatan had the height to back his undoubted skills and belligerent attitude on the field. There was no way that first team coach, Roland Andersson, could miss the tall, noisy forward with the bag full of tricks…

Zlatan's undoubted skills and resolute determination meant that his talents were soon spotted.

Zlatan worked hard to master the flicks, tricks and skills of his hero Ronaldo and practised them every day.

## ZLATAN FACT:

As a 16-year-old, Zlatan spent a week on trial at Queens Park Rangers. The London team decided he was not good enough for them!

# GOING PROFESSIONAL

**Broke and with results going against them, Malmö FF faced a wretched season in 1999. But within their ranks emerged a mercurial talent that took them back to the top.**

**M**almö FF, one of Sweden's greatest clubs, have won the League and Cup double eight times and in 1979 were European Cup runners-up. But in 1999, they were in danger of being relegated for the first time in 63 seasons. With no money to bring in expensive stars, coach Roland Andersson was forced to turn to his younger players.

On September 19, 1999, Malmö needed a draw at Halmstads to avoid the relegation play-offs. With 15 minutes remaining and the score at 1–1, Malmö called on their 17-year-old forward, Zlatan Ibrahimović. Almost immediately he fired a shot that brushed Halmstad's crossbar. But sadly there was no fairy-tale ending. Malmö went down 2–1 and the club were eventually relegated.

For Zlatan, however, it was an exciting time. He came on as sub another five times and in the final match of the season, against Frölunda, struck his first-ever goal. He had really arrived as a player.

As Malmö began their 2000 season in the Superettan (second division), Zlatan soon became their first-choice striker. His first goal came in the third game, against Vasteras. As the team fought their way back to the top division, Zlatan played better and better. He finished the season as Malmö's top scorer with 12 goals from 26 games, as the club gained promotion to the Allsvenskan (first division).

Introducing Malmö FF's new teenage striker. Zlatan made his professional debut in September 1999, aged just 17.

By now, news of his mercurial talent had spread beyond Sweden. The teenager was flown to meet Arsène Wenger at Arsenal, then on to Monaco and Roma, who were all keen to sign him. One club in particular seemed extra determined. Holland's Ajax even sent its sporting director, Leo Beenhakker, to Malmö's training camp in Spain. It wasn't a wasted trip.

In a friendly against Norwegian team, Moss, Zlatan showcased his talents with a glorious goal and Beenhakker reached for his chequebook. For a Swedish record fee of €8.7 million (£7 million), Zlatan was set to join Ajax in the summer of 2001.

"Zlatan fever" swept across Sweden and at his farewell games Zlatan delighted crowds with one extravagant show of skill after another. Meanwhile, the now 19-year-old Zlatan was packing his bags for the land of Johan Cruyff, Marco van Basten and Total Football.

## ZLATAN FACT:

**At the age of 15, Zlatan was ready to give up football and find a job in Malmö's dockyards.**

Arsenal gave Zlatan his own shirt as they tried to tempt him to London.

Thanks to his brilliant skills, goals and flair, "Zlatan Fever" soon took over Sweden.

# AJAX ACE

At Ajax, Zlatan wore Number 9 – the number of the club's legendary striker, Marco van Basten. It was a tough shirt to fill, but in three exciting seasons Zlatan gave supporters some fabulous memories and a taste of the world-class player he was fast becoming.

Thomas Bodström, the Swedish Minister for Justice (and a former professional footballer), had said, "Zlatan is ready for Ajax, the question is whether Ajax is ready for Zlatan." At the Amsterdam Tournament, the annual pre-season friendly, it looked like they were made for each other. Zlatan showed off his skills and wowed his new fans with his interviews.

The fans loved him even more when Zlatan scored the only goal of the game away against bitter rivals Feyenoord early in the season. But things went downhill pretty quickly. His start was marred by injury, suspension and a dip in form. Many of the fans turned against him and he found himself on the bench for some games.

Then, after a bad run of results, coach Co Adriaanse was sacked and replaced by former player Ronald Koeman. Koeman seemed more appreciative of Zlatan's talent, but he still found it difficult to break into the starting line-up. With Ajax now beginning a good run of results, Zlatan was forced to wait patiently for his chance. The Amsterdam team went on to take their first championship in four years. Zlatan had scored only six goals, having started in only 12 of the matches.

At the end of the season Ajax faced Utrecht in the Cup final. A last-minute equalizer sent the game into golden-goal extra-time (where the first team to score wins the match). After five minutes the ball was played to Zlatan. Despite being tightly marked, he chested it down, turned and stretched to pull a shot past the keeper. In his first season he had won "the Double" for Ajax.

## ZLATAN FACT:

In Zlatan's second season at Ajax, he changed the name on his shirt from "Zlatan" to "Ibrahimović".

It took time and persistence, but Zlatan eventually made his mark at Ajax.

On his way to becoming an Ajax legend: in his first season Zlatan helped win "the Double" for Ajax.

**Champions! Zlatan (at the back behind the trophy) celebrates winning the 2004 Dutch league title with Ajax.**

Soon after his return to Ajax after the 2002 World Cup in Japan and South Korea, Zlatan managed to secure his place in the team. He had been helped by another change in staff. Marco van Basten himself had been given a first coaching job with the youth team at Ajax and the Dutch master was also prepared to spend time with Zlatan. He helped rebuild the young striker's confidence and encouraged him to focus on scoring goals. In a fantastic season, Zlatan started to create his own legend, scoring 21 times as Ajax finished runners-up in 2002–03.

Ajax had a strong tradition in European competitions and it brought out the best in Zlatan, too. His Champions League debut against Lyon in September 2002 is remembered as "Zlatan's game". He scored two, including a brilliant 11th-minute strike. He went on to score three more in the tournament as Ajax reached the quarter finals. The adventure continued the following season, with Zlatan hitting two more

in their eight games before Ajax exited in the group stage. Despite being out for some time with his first serious injury, he hit 13 goals as Ajax once again finished as champions.

"Ajax is where I grew up," Zlatan said "where I became a mature person and a great footballer." However, at the start of the 2004–05 season, the Swedish star fell out with club captain Raphael van der Vaart, so Zlatan decided it was time to move on.

But he still had time to leave Ajax fans with a fantastic goodbye present. His goal against NAC Breda in August 2004 was jaw-droppingly sensational.

There was one man who didn't need a showpiece goal to convince him. Fabio Capello had admired Zlatan for a while, and now he sensed his opportunity to sign him. Ever since he was 15, Zlatan had said that he would one day play in Italy. That day had just drawn closer.

No stopping Zlatan. The Ajax striker hit 13 goals in the title-winning season.

# SWEDISH SHINING STAR

**Zlatan had to wait patiently for his opportunity to shine at national level. Then, in Euro 2004, he announced his arrival on the world stage in the most sensational way.**

Zlatan is Sweden's greatest-ever footballer. He is one of only 10 players to play 100 times for his country and is the nation's record goalscorer, averaging more than a goal every two games (56 in 105 appearances). He was entitled to play for Bosnia (his father's birthplace) or Croatia (his mother's home country), but he always wanted to represent the country where he was born and raised.

By January 2001, he had already played for Sweden in an indoor Nordic tournament against Finland and the Faroe Islands. In the spring of that year, while he was in the middle of signing for Ajax, he was selected for the Under-21 team to play against Macedonia in a European Championship qualifier. He scored in a 2–1 victory and netted another in his next match, against Moldova.

With six goals in seven games for the Under-21s, Zlatan showed Swedish national team managers Tommy Söderberg and Lars Lagerbäck that he was ready for the real thing. On October 7, 2001, he made his debut for the national team. He came on as a substitute in a 2002 World Cup qualifier against Azerbaijan and immediately showed what he could do – a back-heeled lob with a clinical finish.

Though he was included in Sweden's squad for the 2002 World Cup in Japan and South Korea, it was clear the 20-year-old was travelling as an understudy. With two minutes to go in Sweden's final group game against Argentina, he finally took to the World Cup stage. He played another 14 minutes in the knockout-round defeat against Senegal – Sweden's World Cup was over.

By the Euro 2004 championships, Zlatan was the star of the Swedish team. At the finals in Portugal, Sweden trounced Bulgaria 5–0 in their opening game. Then came Italy, Zlatan's biggest match yet. With five minutes left, Sweden were trailing 1–0 and struggling to break down the Italian defence. Then Zlatan produced a typical moment of genius (see page 25). All Europe knew his name now.

Zlatan celebrates his outrageously brilliant goal against Italy at Euro 2004.

Zlatan in his first international tournament. He makes a substitute appearance against Senegal in the 2002 World Cup Finals.

Zlatan shields the ball from Denmark's Thomas Helveg at Euro 2004. A draw meant Sweden progressed to the quarter final.

A draw with Denmark ensured Sweden went through to the quarter-finals. The match against the Netherlands was tightly contested, but with no score after extra-time it went to penalties. At 2–2 in the shoot-out, a smiling Zlatan coolly stepped up for his kick. Having had a great tournament, his last kick couldn't have been worse. He blasted the ball over the bar, ending Sweden's best hope of glory in years.

## ZLATAN FACT:

Swedish viewers voted Zlatan Man of Match after their 2002 World Cup tie against Argentina – even though he was sub and came on for only the last two minutes!

# JUVE MARKSMAN

**Juventus had come only third in Serie A in 2003–04. Their reaction was to bring in new coach Fabio Capello and Zlatan Ibrahimović. Over the next two seasons, Juve would lose just five matches...**

On the final day of the 2004 summer transfer window, Zlatan made the move he had always predicted – to Italy. In signing for the country's most famous club, Juventus, he had made a major step up.

His new coach Fabio Capello had paid €19.75 million (£16 million) for a match-winner, not an entertainer, and he vowed to unravel the technique that was the hallmark of Zlatan's Ajax training. Capello demanded less showboating and more assists and goals from the Swede. He sent Zlatan to the gym to build him up and fed him endless balls to hammer into an empty net.

Zlatan flourished under his strict new coach. With Juve's established strike-force of David Trezeguet and Alessandro Del Piero both injured, Zlatan had no time to settle in. But he looked calm and confident from the start. If Ajax had Zlatan the showman, Juve had revealed Zlatan the marksman. He was deadly – strong enough to stay on his feet when jostled by markers, deft enough to drift pass defenders and accurate enough to despatch shot after shot.

He produced a wonderful turn and shot to score on his debut against Brescia, and followed that with some perfect striker's goals – one-on-ones, tap-ins and snapshots through crowded areas. Five goals in his first 10 games saw Juve race to the top of Serie A. By the end of the season, Zlatan had netted 16 goals and as many assists in 35 league games.

In the Champions League, Zlatan began to get a real taste for the big match. Juventus' great run in the competition saw him return to Ajax and play against European giants Bayern Munich and Real Madrid. In the quarter-finals, Juventus met Liverpool. In the first leg at Anfield, Zlatan hit the post with a great shot on the turn, but his team left 2–1 down and their failure to win the home leg meant they went out of the tournament.

As Juventus strolled to the Serie A title, Zlatan was named the Juventus fans' Player of the Year, Italy's Best Foreign Player of the Year, and FIFA's eighth best player in the world. His magical displays had also earned himself a new nickname among the Italian public – "Ibracadabra". It had been a magical season.

For the 2005–06 season Juventus strengthened their squad again, bringing in Patrick Vieira and another striker, Adrian Mutu. Zlatan was now competing with three of the world's greatest forwards for a place in the front line. Juventus started the season winning their first nine games and stayed at the top, closely followed by Milan.

Zlatan worked hard at Juventus to increase the number of goals he scored. It paid off – he netted 16 in his first season.

Zlatan celebrating with David Trezeguet. The Swede's magical displays for Juve saw him nicknamed "Ibracadabra".

Zlatan keeps his eyes on the ball as he prepares to deliver another one of his devastating volleys for Juve.

Zlatan tussling with Inter Milan's Ivan Ramiro Cordoba in November 2004.

Juventus teammates Zlatan and Adrian Mutu celebrate with the 2005 Scudetto trophy.

Zlatan's goalscoring form had dipped, but he often became a provider of goals for others, especially the prolific Trezeguet. He did manage seven goals that season, including a crucial, and classic, goal against Roma.

The defeat of Roma kickstarted Juventus' push for the title. Meanwhile, Zlatan was a vital part of the European campaign. He scored his first Champions League goal against Rapid Vienna with another volley and added another two as the Italian team progressed to a quarter-final against Arsenal. However, Zlatan's disappointing performances as Juventus crashed out again led to accusations that he went missing in the big matches – a claim he would expose as a myth in future years.

Zlatan had proved himself worthy of a place in a team that was getting better and better. Juventus dominated Serie A, finishing with 91 points. They won 27, drew 10 and lost just one league game. They boasted the best attack and best defence, ending the season with an amazing +47 goal difference. The future was bright... or was it?

All season, undercover police had been investigating officials at Juventus and other leading Italian clubs. In a scandal that became known as "Calciopoli", Juventus was found to have rigged games by arranging friendly referees. As a result, the club were stripped of both their 2005 and 2006 titles, and relegated to Serie B for the next season.

When the club's appeals fell on stony ground, Zlatan had to act fast. He had loved his time at Juventus, but to spend a year in the second division, just as his career was in full flow, was unthinkable.

# ZLATAN'S GREAT GOALS PART ONE

A natural inclination to score outstanding goals is what makes Zlatan Ibrahimović such a great player. These following five strikes from 2001–04 are among his best.

## MALMÖ V MOSS
## MARCH 9, 2001

It was only a training camp game, but for Zlatan the stakes could not have been higher; he was in the shop window. He runs onto a ball 3m (10ft) outside the area, chipping it over two defenders. A burst of pace leaves them in his wake and he lobs the ball over the last man. Now, it's the goalie's turn – and he's left standing as a vicious volley flies into the net.

## AJAX V NAC BREDA
## AUGUST 22, 2004

Zlatan at his dribbling best. This is Zlatan's last home game for Ajax. He picks the ball up 30m (98ft) out with his back to goal, but soon turns and heads into the area. As defenders close him down, he slaloms between them, feinting and twisting as he goes. Four of them (one of them twice) are left either on the floor or facing the wrong direction! Then he caps it all by stopping, turning nearly 360 degrees and executing a perfect finish. There is surely no better way to say: "You won't forget me that easily!"

Zlatan reels away in celebration after scoring Eurosport's 2004 "Goal of the Year" for Ajax against NAC Breda.

These two images illustrate Zlatan's incredible goal against Italy at Euro 2004. The strike announced the Swede's arrival on the international scene.

## SWEDEN 1 ITALY 1
## JUNE 18, 2004

Euro 2004, Group C. Sweden have five minutes left to salvage the game. A deep corner from the left is hooked back into the area and the ball pinballs around. Then comes the magic. The ball bounces. Gianluigi Buffon comes to collect it, but Zlatan gets there first. Watching him in real time, it seems impossible. He is facing the wrong way, in mid-air, with a defender on the line still to beat. But somehow avoiding the charging keeper, he twists and flicks the outside of his boot, sending the ball backwards into the top corner. Truly outrageous skill.

# WORLD CUP ADVENTURE

**Sweden went into the 2006 World Cup finals with confidence. With Freddie Ljungberg, Henrik Larsson and their talisman Ibrahimović in the squad, many thought they could match the heroic feats of the 1994 Swedish team and reach the semi-finals.**

Sweden qualified as one of the best group runners-up for the World Cup finals. They scored an average of three goals a game and won all their matches in Group 8, except for two 1–0 defeats against group winners Croatia.

Zlatan got off to a flying start. He scored four in a 7–0 thrashing of Malta in Sweden's first qualifying game. But his most important strike came in Budapest as it began to look like Sweden might not make the finals.

Anything less than a victory in the away tie against Hungary would leave Sweden unlikely to qualify for the tournament. For the entire game, Sweden had huffed and puffed but hadn't been able to break down the Hungarian defence.

Then, on the stroke of 90 minutes, Zlatan, with his back to goal, masterfully controlled the ball on the edge on the area. He turned, brushed his foot over the ball and in an instant had gone past the defender. He had been driven wide of the goal, now he had only the narrowest of angles to whip in a near-post hammer of a shot into the top corner. The ferocity and angle of the shot took the keeper completely by surprise. Sweden had won and Zlatan was going to Germany!

Sweden were drawn in a World Cup group with Trinidad & Tobago, Paraguay and England. Zlatan though, was struggling with an injury. The millions watching around the world were limited to glimpses of Zlatan's genius. His only real chance was a flashed volley that was saved by Trinidad's keeper.

By the time of their third game against England, Zlatan's injury had got much worse. He sat out the match, but a last-minute Henrik Larsson goal sent Sweden through to meet Germany in the knockout stage. Sweden's hopes were still high, but soon disappeared after they went 2–0 down inside 12 minutes. Larsson missed a penalty and Zlatan tried another near-post shot, but that was that – Sweden's World Cup adventure was over.

Henrik Larsson shares the joy after Zlatan puts Sweden 3–0 up against Bulgaria in the 2006 World Cup qualifier.

Zlatan attempts one of his trademark overhead kicks against Trinidad & Tobago at the 2006 World Cup. The game finished goalless.

## ZLATAN FACT:

The Swedes even had a special song for their hero called "Who's Da Man?" Recorded by Elias it stayed at Number 1 in Sweden all summer and was gleefully and continually sung by the thousands of Swedish fans in Germany.

Paraguayan defender Julio Cesar Caceres and Zlatan battle for the ball during a 2006 World Cup match. Sweden eventually won 1–0.

# ZLATAN'S SUPER SKILLS

When you watch Zlatan play, you have to expect the unexpected. Time and time again he produces something astonishing, something different, something spectacular. But what makes him so special?

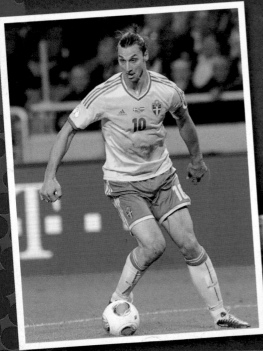

### DRIBBLING
With feints, stopovers, turns and pure pace, Zlatan used to beat man after man, ignoring the calls from his teammates to pass the ball. As his career progressed, Zlatan learned that sometimes there are better options, but he never lost those skills. To the thrill of the fans, he regularly demonstrates them to devastating effect.

## VOLLEYING

The ability to strike the ball in mid-air is one of the most technically difficult footballing skills. It takes agility, spatial awareness, balance and precise timing. Zlatan is so brilliant at volleying it seems as if he has a sixth sense – a mix of incredible improvisation and instinct. He has scored from jaw-dropping distances, from the tightest of angles and – in the greatest goal ever – from unbelievable overhead kicks.

## POWER SHOOTING

Shooting is just another killer weapon in Zlatan's formidable armoury. He's not the only player to stun keepers in this way, but Zlatan combines power with extraordinary accuracy. That's what makes him such a free-kick specialist. Still, you can understand why defenders look a bit nervous standing in the wall!

## THE SCORPION SHOT

Zlatan has demonstrated this amazing technique so many times that the "scorpion shot" has become his signature move. With his back to goal, he twists in mid-air and clips the ball goalwards with his heel. This balletic, taekwondo-inspired action is not just a volley, not just a back-heel and not just a flick, but a breathtaking mixture of all three.

# IN RONALDO'S FOOTSTEPS

**As a teenager, Zlatan never followed a Swedish team. His team, Inter Milan, were 1,500km (930 miles) away in Italy. He idolized their star, Ronaldo, and copied the brilliant Brazilian's moves. Now, in August 2006, he followed in his hero's footsteps and completed a €24.8 million (£20 million) move to the Milan club.**

Inter were the "nearly men". They had come so close, but hadn't won the *Scudetto* (Italian League Championship) for 17 years. The pressure was on head coach Roberto Mancini to succeed and he had picked up Patrick Vieira and Zlatan from Juventus, and Hernan Crespo from Chelsea, to help him.

Zlatan had a dream start for the club. He struck a superb half-volley across the keeper and made an assist for another in his first match against Fiorentina. The team really clicked and Inter went on an incredible record-breaking run of 17 successive victories. Zlatan netted in 11 of them with an amazing array of goals.

He ended his first season as Inter's top goalscorer with 15 goals, but, more importantly, Inter had broken their 17-year league-title drought. The club were runaway champions, finishing the Serie A season with 97 points, yet another record.

Their Champions League campaign was not so successful, though. They crashed out to Valencia in the first knockout game. The following season saw them fare no better, as they were eliminated at the same stage, this time by Liverpool. Despite tasting championship-winning success, Zlatan was collecting only bitter experiences from this competition.

Zlatan's goal against Parma has just won a second successive *Scudetto* for Inter.

Once again Inter set the pace at the top of the league in 2007–08. Then, in March, Zlatan suffered a serious knee injury. The team's form stuttered and Roma closed the gap on them.

The battle for the *Scudetto* came down to the last match of the season. Inter would have to win at Parma – but would they have to do it without Zlatan? He wasn't fit to start, though he did make the bench. Inter struggled for 65 minutes. Then Zlatan entered the fray and the game changed. First he drove a 30m (98ft) shot into the Parma net. Then he followed it with a first-time volley with his weaker left foot. It was sensational.

Named Serie A Player of the Year, Zlatan had proved all his critics wrong. They said he was a troublemaker, but he'd received only two yellow cards all season. They said he wasn't a team player, but the team had suffered badly in his absence. And after the Champions League defeat against Liverpool, they had claimed he didn't have the right temperament for the biggest games. Now he had almost single-handedly won Inter's biggest match for years.

There was one question he hadn't yet answered. Did he score enough goals? Being named top scorer – *capocannoniere* – was a top honour in Italy. Despite missing many matches through injury, Zlatan trailed Alessandro Del Piero by just four goals in 2007–08. As Inter set out for their third successive *Scudetto*, Zlatan also set himself a personal target.

Inter had a new manager for the new season. José Mourinho, Chelsea's self-proclaimed "Special One", took over from Mancini. Zlatan immediately struck up a bond with the new Portuguese coach. He later recalled how Mourinho gave him super-confidence, saying, "From being a cat I felt like a lion."

Inter superstar Zlatan fires home a penalty against PSV Eindhoven in a 2007 Champions League match.

Zlatan fires home an unstoppable volley against Fiorentina in 2006.

Inter continued to play like champions and swept all before them in Serie A. Zlatan's own form was outstanding – his movement on and off the ball, his passing, and, of course, his goals. His back-heel volley against Bologna was voted Goal of the Year. An amazing dribble and chip against Reggina followed and he added a fierce free-kick against Fiorentina which was measured at 109km/h (68mph).

By the last game of the season, against Atalanta, Inter had already been crowned champions for the fourth time. But there was still Zlatan-inspired drama to come. Zlatan was in hot competition for the *capocannoniere* (top scorer) prize. His 12th-minute goal was his 24th of the season. It put him at the top of the scoring chart – but he was level with Marco Di Vaio of Bologna and Genoa's Diego Milito.

With only 10 minutes, left it looked like he'd be sharing the trophy. Suddenly, as he battled for possession in the area, the ball bounced up next to him. Zlatan was facing the wrong direction, but he is, of course, the back-heel expert. With a deft flick of his right foot, he turned to see the ball nestling in the net. He'd done it. He had proved them all wrong again. He was the *capocannoniere*!

Made Player of the Year once more, Zlatan had won all there was to win in Italy. But Inter had missed out on the Champions League again. This time it was Manchester United who prevented them progressing into the quarter-finals. With great teams like United, Chelsea, Real Madrid and the year's winners, Barcelona, taking part, Zlatan wondered whether he would ever fulfil his dream of winning the Champions League.

Zlatan struck up an immediate bond with new Inter coach Jose Mourinho.

## ZLATAN FACT:

In the 2007 Milan derby, Zlatan got to play against his all-time footballing idol, Ronaldo. The Brazilian opened the scoring, but Zlatan got the winner in the second half.

Zlatan celebrates with a fan after victory over Siena means Inter Milan has won the 2006–07 Scudetto.

# ZLATAN'S LIFE OUTSIDE FOOTBALL

There's more than just football in Zlatan's life. Meet Zlatan the family man. A proud dad who loves his sports cars, video games and his secret get-away-from-it-all hobby.

## FAMILY

Like many others who have experienced a chaotic childhood themselves, Zlatan cherishes his family life. He met his partner, Helena Seger, in Malmö in 2001 and in 2006 they had their first son, Maximilian, and two years later his brother Vincent was born. Together with their French bulldog Trustor, they make one happy family.

## GAMING

Zlatan is a self-confessed Xbox addict. As a youth he learned some of his moves from football video games and as a superstar he is the Xbox One ambassador for France. Gaming is his pressure valve, where he can release the tensions and stress of top-level football.

Zlatan loves family life. He met his partner Helena Seger in 2001 and together they have two sons, Maximilian and Vincent.

## CARS

Zlatan loves fast cars – and the faster, the better. His garage is full of the most desirable vehicles in the world. He has an Audi S8, a Maserati Gran Turismo and a collection of Ferraris. But in pride of place are his Lamborghini Gallardo – customized in pink and purple to match his shoes – and his Volvo C30, a relatively modest addition, but Sweden's captain needs a Swedish car!

# WORLD CLASS

**After time away from the national side, Zlatan was back for Euro 2008. Although carrying an injury, he seemed to be in fantastic form and Sweden was relying on him.**

Under Lars Lagerbäck, Sweden had done well to qualify for Euro 2008. They had been without the help of veteran hero Henrik Larsson, who had retired, and without their *Scudetto*-winning hero, Zlatan. Sweden's Player of the Year, who was busy winning his third straight championship with Inter, had missed most of the games after falling out with Lagerbäck after the 2006 World Cup.

Sweden had now made five tournaments in a row, but had failed to impress in any of them. And yet they still dared to dream. Larsson had been persuaded to come out of retirement and Zlatan had ended his self-imposed exile and rejoined the national team with new vigour. He was back and ready to show them what they had missed.

In their opening game against reigning champions Greece, he did just that, producing a man-of-the-match display by constantly testing the Greek defence. The resolute Greece backline held firm until the 67th minute, when Zlatan played a wall pass with Larsson and received the ball back just outside the area. Having won a metre of space, Zlatan coolly looked up and almost effortlessly stroked the ball into the top left corner. It was his first goal in 14 internationals, but what a goal!

His sparkling form continued in the second match, against Spain. A great team going forward, Spain took an early lead. But the Spanish defenders struggled to contain Zlatan's dangerous flicks, passes and mazy dribbles. It was no surprise when he equalized on the half-hour. It was a Zlatan move the fans had seen many times before. He instantly controlled a long cross on the far post. Despite the attentions of two defenders, he had the strength to hold the ball and the calmness under pressure to wait for the moment to pick his shot.

It seemed too good to be true. And it was. Zlatan was still feeling the knee injury that had made him miss many of Inter's games that season. He was substituted at half-time and although the Swedes defended bravely, they lost to a last-minute goal. A half-fit Zlatan turned out for the final group match against Russia, but, playing in pain, he couldn't reproduce his heroics. Sweden's great quest was over for another four years.

Zlatan hit two goals in the 2010 World Cup qualifying campaign, but despite the striker's best efforts Sweden failed to reach the finals and a disillusioned Zlatan announced his retirement from international football.

Sergio Ramos can't prevent the brilliant Zlatan slotting home to equalize against Spain at Euro 2008.

Despite carrying an injury and playing in great pain, Zlatan still made an appearance against Russia at Euro 2008.

Zlatan celebrates getting Sweden's Euro 2008 campaign off the mark with a goal against Greece.

# BARÇA BOUND

In 2009, Zlatan joined Barcelona in a deal worth €66 million (£53 million). It was a match made in heaven. The best team and the best striker in the world. What could possibly go wrong?

The Spanish giants had an unrivalled wealth of talent in players such as Lionel Messi, Andrés Iniesta and Xavi, and had won the treble – the League, Cup and Champions League – in the previous season. Zlatan had reached the very top and he was playing for the greatest club side in the world.

He had some big boots to fill. Striker Samuel Eto'o, who had gone to Inter as part of Zlatan's deal, had scored 36 times in the previous season. But Barcelona, under their manager, Pep Guardiola, had a strict team ethos. No one was bigger than the team and Eto'o had been seen as a disruptive influence.

It started very well. Zlatan set up Messi for a goal on his first start in the Spanish Supercopa and scored on his league debut against Sporting Gijon. He followed up with a goal in each of the next three games, and a brace against Zaragoza made it six strikes from as many games. He capped it all by hitting a volley to win the *Classico* against rivals Real Madrid.

Zlatan had gone to Barça for Champions League success, but that was where things started to go wrong for him. Although he hit two goals at Arsenal in the quarter-finals, his performance was criticized. When he missed the second leg through injury, Messi replaced him in the centre and scored four in a striker's masterclass. Then Mourinho's Inter beat Barca in the semi. And Zlatan's poor performances left him taking a lot of the blame. Once again Zlatan's Champion's League ambitions had come unstuck.

Now something changed in Guardiola's thinking. He began leaving Zlatan out of the team, preferring Messi in the central striking role. He believed Zlatan was too much of an individualist and didn't suit their famous tiki-taka style of football. It was all unravelling fast for the Swede.

Barca strolled on to win *La Liga*. It meant yet another championship for Zlatan. He had scored 16 goals in 29 games. A few were fabulous Zlatan-style efforts, many were putting the finishing touch on typically brilliant Barça passing moves. But it all meant little to the striker.

Zlatan was forced to accept that he would have to move on again. His talents had been appreciated by his teammates and the fans, but the attitude of the coach gave him no alternative.

Zlatan fires home an unstoppable volley against Barcelona's great rivals, Real Madrid, in November 2009.

## ZLATAN FACT:

Zlatan became the first-ever Barcelona signing to score in his first four league matches.

Zlatan's talents were appreciated by his teammates and the fans, but things soon began to go sour for him at Barcelona.

The brilliant Swede scores for Barça against Arsenal in the 2010 UEFA Champions League quarter-final.

# THE RETURN TO ITALY

**Zlatan returns to Italy and Milan, the city of his greatest achievements. But this time it is AC Milan's fans who delight in his goals and celebrate a fantastic *Scudetto* triumph.**

Zlatan left it late to escape Barcelona, but on transfer deadline day 2010 he was back in Milan's San Siro stadium. But this wasn't a return to Inter. He had signed for their city rivals, AC Milan. And this was a different Zlatan, too. He was 29 now – the time most players reach their peak – and had returned from Barcelona a more mature footballer.

There was no debut goal this time. In fact, he missed a penalty in the 2–0 defeat to minnows Cesena. Milan struggled in the first month of the season, but it was Zlatan who took on the role of team leader, encouraging and cajoling his teammates to raise their game.

Zlatan scored his first goals for the club as AC Milan defeated Auxerre in their first Champions League match of the season. Then, his chase and lobbed finish over the Genoa keeper Eduardo gave Milan their first league win, and he went on to inspire a string of triumphs. By the time a Zlatan penalty delivered victory over his former club in the Milan derby, they were top of the table.

Milan had a fine team with a great balance of experience and youth, skill and endeavour. But it was Zlatan who pushed them to the *Scudetto*. His overhead strike against Fiorentina and a powerful shot from the edge of the penalty box against Brescia were among the highlights of his 14 goals and 11 assists.

There could be no doubt now. Zlatan was the King Midas of football. His golden touch brought Milan their first *Scudetto* for eight years – and an incredible eighth successive championship for the Swede.

Could his golden touch help Milan prevail in the Champions League too? It looked possible. He scored four of their six goals in the group stage – one in a draw with his former club, Ajax. But once again his dream would end prematurely. An unexpected defeat at the hands of Tottenham Hotspur sent Milan crashing out of the competition in the first round of the knockout stage.

Zlatan soaks up the adulation after scoring his first goal in a Milan shirt, against Auxerre in the Champions League in 2010.

Despite the previous year's achievements, Zlatan started the 2011–12 season like a man with something to prove. He scored Milan's first goal as they came from behind to beat Inter in the Italian Super Cup and netted AC Milan's first league goal of the season in a 2–2 draw against Lazio. Then he led the line in the Champions League group stage, scoring in four of the six games, including against Barcelona.

Back in Serie A, Zlatan really went to town. From mid-October to the end of January he scored in 13 out of 15 games. His first goal of a brace against Chievo was his 100th in Serie A. The cheekiest of back-heels, the kind that only Zlatan can pull off, helped sink Novara. Only a suspension after a red card for slapping a Napoli player halted his run.

And so to unfinished business – the Champions League – and Zlatan was on a mission. Against Arsenal he set up both of Robinho's goals and earned himself a penalty, which he slotted home. The 4–0 scoreline was enough to see Milan through to a quarter-final against Barcelona. Could this be the ultimate sweet revenge for Zlatan?

Zlatan is congratulated by teammate Mathieu Flamini after scoring a penalty against city rivals Inter Milan in November 2010.

Coming back from suspension like he'd never been away, Zlatan smashed a hat-trick against Palermo and kept scoring. With five in the next seven games and then two against Siena, he passed his previous season's record of 25 goals, finishing the season with 28 goals in 32 matches. He was crowned *capocannoniere* once more.

Milan were level with Juventus at the top of the table. If they were to win the *Scudetto* again, they needed to win their last-but-one league game against Inter. Zlatan had led the team this far, but could he see the job through? Inter took the lead, but Zlatan equalized from the penalty spot just before half-time. Forty seconds into the second half, Zlatan took a superb touch at the edge of the box, skipped past his marker and lobbed the keeper. But football isn't a fairy tale. Inter regrouped and came back to win 4–2 and the *Scudetto* went to Juventus.

Zlatan's incredible run of championship triumphs had finally come to an end. It was a double disappointment because, despite Zlatan's best efforts, Milan had exited the Champions League at the hands of Barcelona. It clearly hurt the great Swede.

Zlatan was now 30 years old. He had won every domestic honour in Italy. He could stay at Milan and have another crack at the Champions League or he could embark on one last epic adventure. Naturally Zlatan chose the excitement of the unknown...

## ZLATAN FACT:

Zlatan celebrated Milan's 2011 *Scudetto* victory with a perfectly executed kick to his teammate Antonio Cassano's head – while the midfielder was giving a live TV interview! It was just for fun and Cassano wasn't hurt!

A creator of chances for others, Zlatan shows off his passing skills against Catania Calcio in November 2011.

The Sweden and AC Milan striker celebrates scoring against his old club Barcelona in November 2011.

# ZLATAN'S GREAT GOALS PART TWO

When Zlatan's at his ingenious and glorious best, even the world's best defenders have little chance of stopping him. "Audacious", "remarkable" and "outrageous" describe this stunning selection of goals.

## INTERNAZIONALE 2 BOLOGNA 1 OCTOBER 4, 2008

This Goal of the Season came in the very first league game of the season! Adriano sprints down the touchline and fires over a thigh-high, fierce cross. Zlatan and his marker race to meet the ball at the near post. The defender appears to have run the race as he stoops to head away. But before head meets ball, a foot appears. It's Zlatan's heel. It doesn't move but waits for the ball and diverts it with stunning accuracy past the keeper. Once again, Zlatan seems to have defied the laws of geometry with an audacious finish.

## INTERNAZIONALE 2 PALERMO 0 NOVEMBER 15, 2008

Judging by the look on his face after this nestles in the net, Zlatan loved this one. He's on the ball on the right about 20m (66ft) from goal. He has options: a far post cross or a short incisive pass inside the area are both on. But not this time. Zlatan puts his foot over the ball, rolls it a metre forwards and unleashes a thunderbolt. The keeper doesn't even flinch. It's a blur as it arcs through the air, brushes the inside of the far post and ruffles the back of the net. That's precision engineering executed at 124km/h (77mph).

Zlatan celebrates a goal against Bologna. Scored in the first game of the season, the goal was later declared the "Goal of the Season".

Pulling the trigger – Zlatan is about to blast home against Palermo in November 2008. The shot was recorded at having reached 124km/h (77mph).

## MILAN 3 BRESCIA 0
## DECEMBER 4, 2010

This is pure cruelty to defenders. They've got him surrounded in the area, but Zlatan doesn't panic. He drags the ball back outside the area and stops. When Zlatan is at his best he can make time stand still. It's as if he's giving the opposition time to regroup. He looks up. Ready? OK. Here I go! He has a quick look up at the four players positioned in front of him, nudges the ball to the right and blasts an unstoppable bullet of a shot inside the near post. What a tease! What a goal!

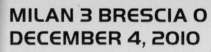

Another memorable goal, this time for Milan. He seemed to make time stand still before drilling an unstoppable shot home against Bresica in 2010.

# ZLATAN'S TEAMMATES

**For all his individual talent, Zlatan has always understood that football is a team game. Fortunately, he has been lucky enough to play alongside the best...**

## HENRIK LARSSON

Separated by a decade in age, Henrik Larsson and Zlatan both grew up in the Skane region of Sweden, were nurtured in Holland, played at Barcelona and are national heroes. They first played together for Sweden in 2004 and soon became firm friends. Over three tournaments, the national team could boast two world-class forwards until Larsson retired, after winning his 106th cap, in 2009. Zlatan acclaims Henrik as his mentor, while Larsson returns the compliment, saying, "The truth is that as a striker he has it all."

## LIONEL MESSI

"Messi is extraordinary," Zlatan has said. "He does things only seen in video games." People expected great things when Zlatan teamed up with Messi at Barcelona, but unfortunately it just didn't happen for them. While Zlatan struggled at his new club, the Argentinian was winning his first-ever FIFA World Player of the Year Award. Zlatan likes Messi a lot and thinks they could still work magic together. In fact, he has urged PSG to reunite them.

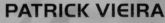

### PATRICK VIEIRA

Zlatan had already been at Juventus for a year when Patrick Vieira arrived in 2005. They both had strong characters, an indefatigable determination and they were both winners. Their partnership was an integral part of Juventus' 2005–06 championship-winning team. When the *Calciopoli* scandal broke, Vieira left for Inter Milan, which helped Zlatan make the decision to take the same journey. Vieira's playing time at Inter was curtailed by a run of injuries, but he remained an inspirational member of the triple *Scudetto*-winning squad.

# THE PRIDE OF PARIS

**A new club and a new adventure for Zlatan. But it's the same old story of success – great goals, player of the year and more League winners' medals.**

There were a hundred clubs who would have snapped up the chance of signing Zlatan. But he chose Paris Saint-Germain (PSG). The club had just been taken over by new super-rich owners who hoped the club could dominate Europe. This was the adventure that Zlatan was seeking.

Zlatan loves to score on his debut, but found himself on the PSG bench for the first game of the season. No matter. He came on and scored twice to salvage a 2–2 draw. Zlatan was in town. Goals came in a torrent. Two in PSG's first win. Another two in a draw with deadly rivals Marseilles. And a hat-trick at Valenciennes – all before Christmas.

If Zlatan was hungry for domestic success, it was nothing to his desire for Champions League glory. But in the quarter-finals, PSG came up against Barcelona, arguably the greatest club side ever. Despite Zlatan scoring in a 2–2 draw against his former club, PSG were knocked out on away goals.

As PSG swept to their first Championship in 19 years, Zlatan was awarded another Player of the Year award. He ended the season as Ligue 1's top goalscorer with 30 goals. Into his second season, Zlatan just seemed to get better and better. Not only was he scoring freely, but nearly all of those goals were spectacular. In the Champions League, Zlatan scored 10 goals, including four in one game against Anderlecht, as PSG reached another quarter-final. His searing left-foot shot from outside the area had helped demolish Leverkusen in the previous round. Now they faced Chelsea. Zlatan had helped his team to a 3–1 first leg victory, but sitting it out with an injury in the return, he could only look on helplessly as a late goal sent PSG out.

As PSG strode on towards a second Ligue 1 victory in 2013–14, Zlatan's name was at the top of both the scorers' and the providers' chart. He hit 26 league goals (a club record for goals in a season) and 41 goals

in all competitions, with many claiming his scorpion goal against Bastia was his best ever. He ended the season as Ligue 1's Player of the Season for the second consecutive year.

He started the 2014–15 season in ominous form too, scoring both of PSG's goals in a 2–0 victory over Guingamp in the season-opening Trophée des Champions, his first silverware of the season. His first hat-trick of the season (against St Etienne) arrived before the end of August. But this was not a smooth season for Zlatan. PSG may have marched to the domestic title, but Zlatan was in and out of the side through injury, making only 24 appearances – albeit scoring 19 goals.

He played a significant role in PSG's progress in the Champions League, though. This was the one trophy PSG wanted above all others. They finished second in the group (behind Barcelona, who they beat, without an injured Zlatan, at home). Their reward was a round-of-16 tie against Chelsea.

Still struggling with an injury, Zlatan watched on from the stands as PSG drew the first leg 1–1 in Paris. He returned for the second leg, but was controversially sent off in the 31st minute in London. It mattered not: PSG produced a memorable rearguard performance to draw the match 2–2 and progress on away goals. Banned for one match, he missed the 3–1 home quarter-final defeat to Barcelona and, returning for the second leg, could do little to avert a 2–0 loss at the Nou Camp. Zlatan's Champions League dream would have to wait for another season.

But that wasn't PSG's final shot at silverware for the season. In April, Zlatan scored twice as PSG defeated Bastia 4–0 in the Coupe de la Ligue final. For Zlatan, the season might not have run to the perfect script, but at least he had proved that, when fit, he was still one of the world's very best players.

On the ball against Olympique de Marseilles in October 2012. Zlatan received the "Player of Year" in his first season in France.

## ZLATAN FACT:

PSG signed Zlatan from Milan for €20 million (£16 million). In terms of combined transfer fees that made him the most expensive footballer in the world, with a career total of €180 million (€146 million).

Zlatan won a third consecutive league championship-winner's medal in 2014–15 in addition to the domestic cup double.

# ZLATAN'S GREAT GOALS PART THREE

Even as Zlatan moves towards the end of his playing career, the quality of his goals do not diminish. In fact, they may actually be getting better!

This pinpoint, acrobatic volley against France at Euro 2012 was impossible for the keeper, Hugo Lloris, to save.

## SWEDEN 2 FRANCE 0
## JUNE 19, 2012

Sweden were already eliminated from Euro 2012, but Zlatan hadn't finished with the competition. He was in a central position a metre inside the area when Seb Larsson's chipped cross came from the right. Effortlessly leaning back in thin air, Zlatan swivelled so that his legs were almost parallel to the ground. Stretching his foot around the advancing defender, Philippe Mexes, Zlatan volleyed a diagonal shot across the goal. It arced past the diving keeper, hit the ground just before it crossed the line and nestled in the far corner of the net. Acrobatic, accurate and simply amazing.

## BAYER LEVERKUSEN 0 PSG 4
## FEBRUARY 18, 2014

When PSG met Bayer Leverkusen in the first knockout stage of the 2014 Champions League, Zlatan dominated the game; scoring a penalty and controlling play all over the field. His second goal was a gem. He picked up the ball outside the area, played it wide and when it finally was passed back to him, he hit a 20-metre belter, clocked at 103km/h – with his weaker, left, foot! The ball seemed to defy physics and actually increase its velocity as it sped with unerring accuracy to the top corner of the goal.

Zlatan dazzled against Bayer Leverkusen in the Champions League in 2014. His second goal was an astonishing 20-metre thunderbolt.

## NICE 2 PSG 1
## DECEMBER 1, 2012

Zlatan placed the ball almost dead centre on the arc of the penalty area. There was a nine-man wall, including two PSG players. His face was a picture of concentration. Everyone knew what was going to happen next. He was going to hit it hard, very hard indeed. And he did. Somehow he found a gap and suddenly the ball was trying to tear a hole through the inside netting. This blockbuster was measured at 180km/h (112mph) – one of the fastest shots ever recorded – but it was also perfectly accurate. And completely unstoppable.

A trademark blockbuster from Zlatan against Nice was measured at 180kph (112mph) – one of the fastest shots ever recorded.

The England players could only look on as Zlatan unleashed the "Goal of the Century" – his acrobatic, outside-of-the-area overhead kick.

# THE GOAL OF THE CENTURY

On 12 November 2012, Sweden played England at Friends Arena in Stockholm, and Zlatan Ibrahimović marked the stadium's debut with all four goals in a 4–2 win. The last was one of the best ever seen.

## SWEDEN 4 ENGLAND 2
## 14 NOVEMBER 2012

They called it the "Goal of the Century". Zlatan had already bagged himself a hat-trick in the just-opened Friends Arena, but he was hungry for something else – something sensational. When England's keeper weakly headed the ball out of the area, the opportunity arrived. Impossible? Zlatan had to chase the falling ball down and he was still 30m (98ft) out. Technical? He had to perform the perfect bicycle kick to get the distance and trajectory right. Audacious? No one, even Zlatan's greatest fans, imagined even he could attempt such a shot. Fantasy football!

# CAPTAIN ZLATAN

**Persuaded out of international retirement – he admitted he had missed wearing the shirt – and this time proudly leading Sweden out as captain, Zlatan dazzled spectators at Euro 2012.**

On August 14, 2010, when Sweden played a friendly against Scotland, Zlatan made his second debut for the national team. New coach Erik Hamrén had persuaded him to return – and had given him the captain's armband.

Sweden progressed steadily through the qualifying rounds. Zlatan scored two in a 6–0 thrashing of San Marino and a hat-trick in 20 minutes as they put five past Finland. However, the Swedes succeeded in making the finals only by beating Netherlands in the last match. Zlatan was forced to sit this out due to suspension after collecting two yellow cards.

In the finals in Poland and Ukraine, Sweden would again disappoint, but this time Zlatan really made the world sit up and watch. His first goal in the tournament, against hosts Ukraine, was a typical piece of close-to-goal, clinical finishing. But it was his second, against France, that left millions around the world watching open-mouthed.

Zlatan's acrobatic volley – later named goal of the tournament – topped off a magnificent series of displays. He worked as hard as anyone, tackled back and was still there to provide the final shot or pass. As captain he led by inspiration and by persuasion. Zlatan was voted into the Euro 2012 Team of the Tournament – the only player from a team that didn't make the quarter-finals.

After the Euros, Zlatan continued to inspire the Swedish national team. In the opening match at

Captain Zlatan opened his Euro 2012 goalscoring account by scoring against co-hosts Ukraine.

Zlatan heads home against Portugal in the 2014 World Cup play-off, but it isn't enough for Sweden to progress to the finals in Brazil.

Sweden's new Friends Arena in November 2012, Zlatan scored all four goals in a 4–2 triumph over England. He stabbed home the first with a lightning reaction. The second was a perfectly controlled chest-down followed by a stunning volley. The third was a drilled free kick and the last an audacious, flying overhead kick from outside the box and one of the greatest goals ever.

It was no fluke. In the same stadium he hit another glorious hat-trick in a friendly against Norway. In the World Cup 2014 qualifiers, with Sweden trailing 4–0 to Germany, a Zlatan goal inspired an amazing comeback to 4–4. He then hit another five goals in qualification as Sweden fought their way into a play-off against Portugal.

Portugal had a 1–0 lead from the first leg and when Ronaldo gave Portugal a two-goal advantage in Stockholm, it looked desperate for Sweden. Still, Zlatan never gave up. He headed home from a corner, then rifled in a free-kick. He gave everything, but couldn't prevent Ronaldo grabbing two late goals to take Portugal through to the finals. "It was probably my last attempt to reach the World Cup with the national team," reflected Zlatan, "but one thing is for sure – a World Cup without me is nothing to watch!"

Zlatan leads from the front again as Sweden begin their Euro 2016 qualifying campaign against Austria in Vienna.

# ZLATAN SAYS...

Ask Zlatan a straight question and you'll get a honest answer. He shoots from the hip – sometimes ultra-confident, sometimes mischievous and often very, very funny...

**"YOU BOUGHT A FERRARI BUT YOU DRIVE IT LIKE A FIAT."**
On being badly treated at Barcelona

**"IT'S ZLATAN-STYLE."**
When asked if his playing style was Swedish or Yugoslavian

**"NOTHING, SHE ALREADY HAS ZLATAN."**
When asked what Zlatan bought his future wife for her engagement present

Zlatan celebrates his third goal against England in November 2012. His eventual four goals opened Sweden's new national stadium in style.

"I CAN PLAY IN THE ELEVEN POSITIONS BECAUSE A GOOD PLAYER CAN PLAY ANYWHERE ON THE PITCH."

"THERE ARE A FEW MOMENTS I WILL SEE ON THE INTERNET WHEN I RETIRE AND I'LL TELL MYSELF THEY'RE AMAZING. I'LL ASK MYSELF HOW EVEN I COULD HAVE ACHIEVED SUCH FEATS."

Two great players: Zlatan and Cristiano Ronaldo congratulate one another after the 2014 World Cup play-off first leg.

# ZLATAN – THE COACHES' VIEW

Zlatan said in 2014. "If you talk to the coaches I have played for, the only one that would say maybe I was a problem was Pep Guardiola. [That is] if he has something to say, which I don't find he has." He doesn't. But all the others sure do...

> "I DON'T UNDERSTAND WHEN PEOPLE SAY HE IS A DIFFICULT GUY TO WORK WITH OR A DIFFICULT PERSONALITY. WHEN YOU HAVE SOMEBODY THAT IS A WINNER AND WANTS TO WIN ALL THE TIME, I THINK HE IS VERY, VERY EASY... I RATE HIM AS ONE OF THE BEST PLAYERS I HAVE EVER COACHED."
>
> José Mourinho

José Mourinho and Zlatan worked together at Inter Milan and have a great respect for one another.

> "IBRAHIMOVIĆ IS A REALLY GOOD PLAYER WHO CAN DECIDE A TOP-LEVEL GAME IN A SINGLE MOMENT."
>
> Fabio Capello

Zlatan has continued to flourish under manager Lauren Blanc at Paris Saint-Germain.

"IBRAHIMOVIĆ IS A PHENOMENON, WHEN HE PLAYS ON THIS LEVEL, HE'S IMPOSSIBLE TO MARK."

Roberto Mancini

"IS ZLATAN BETTER THAN MESSI AND RONALDO? RIGHT NOW, I'D SAY HE IS."

Arsène Wenger

"HE DOES NOT SURPRISE ME. HE CONFIRMS IN EVERY MATCH THAT HE IS AN EXTRAORDINARY COMPETITOR AND ABOVE ALL, HAS THE ABILITY TO MAKE MOVES THAT OTHER PLAYERS CANNOT."

Laurent Blanc, PSG coach

# AMAZING ZLATAN

Wherever he goes, Zlatan scores goals, wins titles and breaks records. The list of his achievements goes on and on...

Four-goal hero Zlatan holds the match ball aloft following PSG's 5-0 victory of Anderlecht in the Champions League in 2013.

Zlatan celebrates scoring at Euro 2012. Will Zlatan get the chance to replicate his club success on the international stage?

# ZLATAN FACTS

**Birth Date:** October 3, 1981
**Birth Place:** Malmo, Sweden
**Height:** 6' 5" (1.95m)
**Weight:** 95 kg

428 Total league appearances
244 Goals
92 Assists
11 League titles
48 goals from 98 appearances for Sweden

# ZLATAN RECORDS

Only player to have won eight consecutive league titles (in ESP/ITA/NED with 5 different teams)
Combined Career Transfer Fee €180m (£146m)
Only player to have won 4 different national Super Cups (1 NED, 3 ITA, 2 ESP, 1 FRA)
Only player to score in De Klassieker (Ajax v Feyenoord), *El Classico* (Barça v Real Madrid), Catalan Derby (Barça v Espanyol), Milan Derby (AC Milan v Inter), Turin Derby (Juventus v Torino), Derby d'Italia (Inter v Juventus), *Le Classique* (PSG v Marseilles), *"El Cashico"* (PSG v Monaco)
Only player to have scored with 6 different teams in Champions League
Most UEFA EURO Tournaments with at least 2 goals – (2004, 2008, 2012)
9 *Guldbollen* (Swedish Footballer of the Year)
Euro 2012 Goal of the Tournament (vs France)

# ZLATAN HONOURS

## NETHERLANDS

2 x *Eredivisie* League titles
1 x KNVB Cup
1 x Dutch Super Cup
1 x *Eredivisie* "Goal of the Year" (vs NAC Breda)

## SPAIN

1 x *La Liga* Championship
2 x Spanish Super Cups
1 x UEFA Super Cup
1 x FIFA Club World Cup

## ITALY

6 x Consecutive Serie A league titles – Serie A record
3 x Serie A "Player of the Year" – Serie A record
5 x Serie A "Foreign Player of the Year" – Serie A record
2 x Serie A top scorer – Serie A record (only player to do with two different Serie A teams)
17 x consecutive Serie A wins with Inter Serie A record
3 x Italian Super Cups and 1 x Super Cup runners-up
1 x Serie A Goal of the Year (2008 – v Bologna)

## FRANCE

3 x Ligue 1 Championship
2 x Ligue 1 Player of the Year
2 x Ligue 1 top scorer
2 x French Super Cup
1 x Coupe de la Ligue
1 x Coupe de France

## SWEDEN NATIONAL TEAM

Highest all-time scorer (56 goals)
Man of the Match in three successive Euro tournaments: v Italy (Euro 2004), v Greece (Euro 2008), v France (Euro 2012)
Highest UEFA European Championships Swedish top scorer
Only Swedish Player to score in three separate UEFA European Championships
Highest All-Time Swedish Champions League scorer

*NOTE: All statistics are up to date as of the end of August 2015.*

# CREDITS

The publishers would like to thank the following sources for their kind permission to reproduce the pictures in this book. The page numbers for each of the photographs are listed below, giving the page on which they appear in the book and any location indicator (T-top, B-bottom, L-left, R-right).

Zlatan shows off his superb ball-control skills in a World Cup qualifier against Malta in June 2009.

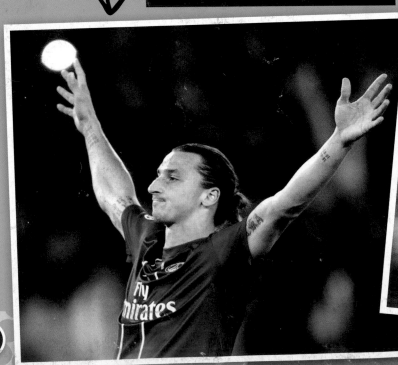

There's only one Zlatan! The Swedish superstar celebrates after scoring yet another goal, this time against Dynamo Kiev in 2012.